UNDERGROUND SUN

Lee Edward Pricer

NeoPoiesisPress.com

NeoPoiesis Press, LLC

2775 Harbor Ave SW, Suite D, Seattle, WA 98126-2138
Inquiries: Info@NeoPoiesisPress.com
NeoPoiesisPress.com

Lee Edward Pricer - Underground Sun
ISBN 978-0-9975021-1-4 (paperback: alk. paper))

    1. Poetry. I. Pricer, Lee Edward. II. Underground Sun.

Library of Congress Control Number: 2017931355

First Edition

Cover Design: Milo Duffin and Stephen Roxborough

Printed in the United States of America.

for the Halibot

Contents

ConScience

never one to cling to the confines of the flesh
he wipes the sweaty condensation of beaded
petri dish research
on his white scientist lapel
as he paints abstract
with diseased needles
through nearsighted microscopes
storing his art in formaldehyde mausoleums
as he searches for potions to postpone his own mortality
because he's not quite ready to stop looking for the
Science in God
but like a starving klepto
growing a conscience
rivaling the size of his cancer
he's done stealing time

9 to 5 (in)voluntary manslaughter

8:48 am:
Him -What the fuck are you looking at?
Panhandler - An endangered Species.

8:56 am:
Walking through a Revolving window glass door
chainsaw hope killer
sporting Armani with alligator skin briefcase corner teeth
the dead Darwinian champion swinging in his left
soy latte virtually sucked dry in his right
he climbs the Rise on conveyor-belts
disguised as elevators slash escalators
drowning out the unbearable buzz of the business beehive
in a malnutritioned apple black iwhatever
crowd surfing imaginary out stretched skeleton bones
the 1000's of Willie Loman arms holding him up

Singing the chorus out of tune

"Music our last Aphrodisiac,
Music our last Aphrodisiac…"

And the hypnotic bass line spurs aimless probing
causing an alien abduction in his thinking:

Democracy killed the worker bee
Freedom killed the economy
My Ivy League Education taught me
How to work less for more money

And now

We're just arboreal middle-aged monkeys
Swinging in evolution's digestive tract without trees
Killing ourselves with our own toys
Time for the championship title game

NASA's pink pepto bismol vs. Self Destruction
missile pinball

Vegas Bookie answer –
"If you're betting on that dog race, always bet on the hare

Because the way I see it man's become lactose intolerant--
Time to colonize a galaxy a little less milky."

He said, blatantly misquoting Stephen William Hawking

9:00 am
Enter Cubicle
Shut down Cerebral Cortex
Turn on computer
And Survive till

5:00 pm
Involuntary Manslaughter

yah

never wanting to suffer the toothless mutterings of
fatherhood
he bore children just to eat their placentas.
to sample his own ancestry
to reincarnate his own history
and in the drool of a newborn mouth
he finds a hint of his lost self
in bone marrow and pheromones
left on sultry aftertaste breath remains
spewing from the dizzying rainbow
cataclysmic orgasm in which it came
leaving the many open and sored legs of octopus mothers
showcasing purple eggplant veins
the remnants of living blood
false advertising their death-way to Earth's soil
like broken roots
to rear childhood dreams
from android recipes
in sacrificial homage breastfed
through catheter cords
of umbilical skylights
point blue on blue eyes up
through blurry entrails
of an underwater uphill birth—

to taste his own ancestry

courted by beasts for long ago now

courted by beasts for long ago now
I believe
somewhere an alien cries
more than vermin
more than sperm
watched over under pregnant eyes

bathed in iris white

escaped in permanent holiday
mistletoe be the suns
plucked and fed
bittersweet kisses
of evolutionary phases

black night handkerchiefs borrowed
skies wiped full
in naked regalia

stonewashed

stonewashed but unclean
there's a hole in your jeans
somewhere around the knees

the tired skin pokes through
blood scabbed and scraped
like pantyhose it's got a run
multiple overdoses in praying

and your Jesus tatts are like nicotine patches
false advertisements of faith
sundried and faded
no needle to bring back the color
and your fear breeds a detectable odor
as you sweat through the look
in a nervous tick at double checks
at phantom wrist watches never there

no need for time
never was

one of many premature preparations for dying

stonewashed but unclean
there's a hole in your dream

& if you don't feel like falling

see the world again
through orphan eyes

Fatherless & Motherless

same substance down to the core

singing your own sad

singing your own sad

home

a front porch chime
without the wind
left lost and scared
tried to ride the breeze
but it brought you back

sweet science in the alibi
domestic violence
thought he'd try it

nurture gave way to nature
head turned a swivel twitch
a 3rd eye cycloptic tick

you ride the echoing wave screams
a back lash whip of premature slaves

home

a front porch lamp
without the light
left lost and scared
tried to ride the dawn
but the dark brought you back
sweet science in the alibi

so the lullaby goes

in the shadow
the shadow
the place where nothing grows
you lost yourself young

in the shadow
the shadow
the place where nothing grows
you found yourself old

home

a front porch chime
without the wind
left lost and scared
what have you done?

sweet science in the alibi
domestic violence thought he'd try it
nurture gave way to nature
head turned a swivel twitch
a 3rd eye ecliptic tick

you ride the distorted screams
eradicated in a dislocated jaw

so the lullaby goes

home

a front porch mother with a black eye
a halfhearted smile without a wave goodbye
left lost and scared
empty shopping carts on their side
brown bag covered songs
poured into ulcered dreams

so the lullaby goes

in the shadow
in the shadow
the place where nothing grows
you found yourself young

in the shadow
in the shadow
the place where nothing grows
you found yourself old

in the shadow
the place where nothing grows
you found yourself home

singing your own sad
/yah/yah/yah

anticipatory dread

I've watched heathens drool
as their cyanide saliva drips
off their sharpest tooth
like burning light off - the tip of a

<pre>
          c
             r
                e
                   s
                   c
                e
          n
       t
  moon
</pre>

anticipatory dread in abominable wretchedness
born, to be aborted
it cackles its way out of superstition in catatonic laughs
of hyperbolic hyenas conjuring black comedy out of failed
attempts in finding never-ends from never-wheres

and crazy is.... the mother merry matriarch of imagination
that hyper-extends its apparitional claws to comb
the hospital smell out of unconditioned hair

and crazy is... the black eyed will of the creature that wants
nothing, but to eats its own pupils

and crazy is...deep down, wanting the bite

rusty bikes in an automobile world

bronze eggbeater spokes kick up the dirt
to scramble the past
with atrophied quadriceps, hamstrings, and calves

these anaerobic strokes of rusty bicycles
riders riding bareback on old iron horse trails
the rubber white walled wheels playing hopscotch
on old concrete covered rails

East to West some hungry pedal
West to East, backwards, a few they struggle

but all chase
the shrinking horizon in high-low pressured circles
playing
duck, duck, goose
with the closest star
until the wick almost gone

they fight

one by one through polluted scar skies
cracking open almonds
the brown of Los Angeles sunsets
overwhelming underused retinas

to feast on its white insides

to become blind
in and a part

of the fading type of light

dinner

sitting down at the table

legs enveloped under the chair
postmarked today

his hair was

fallin'

rainin' brunette promises

broken

the lonely strands they were

findin'

the h o l e s

the fingers of a silver antique fork

he was eatin'

himself

and what a skinny man he was

thinkin'

he had some special burden

thinkin'

somehow he was hurtin'

more

& I said

like an unbidden simpleton:

"Join the race man,
you's just human"

but of course
he chose to ignore

grinnin'

given me some salty pirates glare

his heart barely beatin'

a ssssslllooowww drrabbb drrruuummmm
in a skin draped tightly like a snare

a white ribbed cage

elevatin'

up

&

down

breathin'

that delicious last breath

he was eatin'

himself

and what a hungry man he was

backyard ballads

the horizon pants
we listen closely

its wind plays equestrian with the trees
conifers, open leaves, brush in jubilee
no synthesizer could birth it better
no background cancer could quiet its banter

breath

Earth

in every gust

just us

life

dust

snowing in the sun

did it ever taste any better?

caterpillars crunching
chlorophyll crackers
carbon copies of mimes
thrown away minutes kept
in feta and wine
half eaten teasings
home
aviators sing
lost for paths
imaginations migrate
in ballads of the backyard

come to close
close to come

blue cars streak past
intermittent
dreadlocks of time

listen closely

they play to tune

waves breaking in the Adriatic
far off aqua musings of
the Mediterranean in June

come to close
close to come

the horizon pants
we listen closely

breath

Earth

in every gust

just us

life

dust

snowing in the sun

come

on guard to the vanguard

Paul, the burier's, sweaty hands slip
slip on the silver frame of maple chests

should have worn the white gloves
shouldn't have had an ice stare for traction
but fingerprints were more important
in a death that needs responsibility
they cheer

On guard to the vanguard!

Degeneration Y has its claims
in white star shaped derivatives
running red through the blue veins
comatose allegiance pledged
by virgins stifled as their love
                              was taken out of drugs
no prophylactic for mental illness
paranoia in a staring contest
                              easy to win
when you induce the twitch

On guard to the vanguard!

in new found patience taught to the Patriot
a half screwed back pocket flask drips
              horizontal rain
in a long walk against the grain

you can turn the other cheek like me

but there's no punch like a double amputee's
   trust me
in a bested effort to clean the streets

an army of one can try to wish away,

but it's too fucking easy to see

On guard to the vanguard!!!

antennas on our heads
bugs in the teeth
your weapons used back
in a Hitchcock-eyed ending
we'll get off on your cowboy face in the demise
rubbing sticks on the plutonium in your peace pipe
spitting stock piled stomach acid from hunger strikes
to lunger in your empty black commander and chief
coffee cup

handle ripped off
disintegrating

Drink up!

in the beginning of the end

On guard to the vanguard!

Paul, the burier's, sweaty hands slip

bones

her smiles seem like relics to me
a stalwart oasis of what time ought to be

quilts made of empathy
     ecstasy
  afghans for sleeping eyes
    how I covet both
but witches wear the time exposed
  like jewelry on decomposing bones

and the wonders
they fare inside of me
  like windows on a helpless soul

and what we un-see
is what we believe
    of angels that we grow

empty blankets slide down
slivers of the rental moon meddle in awakening
broken eyelashes of the patriarch

those slanted smiles
    they seem
   like relics to me
a picture frozen
a blister
a stalwart oasis
of what time ought to be

jewelry on decomposing bones

yes wherever you go...

home just jewelry on decomposing bones

oasis

attached in salt water taffy

may the soul not worry

for without much rest

it is weary,

and fear not these barnacles only

they live underwater

in a desert oasis

etched in pencil on a famous author's easel

pages of which blanket a cold heart breaking

underground

and buried

rickshaw

Q: What will be done?
A: What will be done.

the answer came like
spontaneous combustion
in a pain-free yell
as an old one legged man arrived again
with a soot covered whistle
commandeering
a wooden accordion covered rickshaw
mounted
            on rhombus wheels

ask him, and I'm sure if he'd reply
he'd call it
the devils taxi—
without the fare

as this with others his arrivals came and went with
the Sundays
as so did my trips to the trapezoid church
became more and more reoccurring
yet
more and more un-assuring

uncomfortable as always is the trek
but deep down
I know
it has to be

and with bumps coming from slanted square wheels
I see bent
            like religious walls
the captain's old organic leg stealing weight from me and
his black flamingo painted false

        he was struggling with the load
    as once too maybe he was a demon
carrying now
only the sins of those...
                        feather souls
        looking for homes
in rising parachute angels
the white jellyfishes
without the burden of ripcords
or without the necessity of air

and me

1000 days from the fall
                up
                I
in a backwards count
on a beaten horse
still know nothing
but the ride

am eagerly awaiting

the next trip

split fare queen chameleon

the checkmate
yellow black chessboard
of slamming side door cab confessions
leaves me a tipped king
as she walks,
a split fare queen chameleon,
across my mind
in party dress

the holey stocking knee high
stiletto
silhouette of a soul-mate

her familiar
becomes
less and less

the more she wears

the garden

somehow he could see through
the blond hair draped over his eyes
that he was going to die young

his fascination with yellow went well beyond
his taste for women
which if nothing else was the explanation for
a daily meandering through the forever
hillside of mustard grass

his neon shoelaces helped to
blaze a trail through the
marmalade maze of a golden field
to a special garden he had prepared
long ago

while he took off his clothes
piece by piece
he forced himself to think about her scream
as to make sure that the pitch
and tone were identical to his
for the dark night was
the murder of not only the innocent
but the murder of his conscience

and as the bright mango sun beat down
over the long stalks of his dandelion garden
he couldn't help but ponder the lemony irony
of how beautiful a weed could be---

(In his heart he always dreamt he was a dandelion.)

as now he was naked about to lie supine
amongst his fellow dandelion
he opened an envelope
he'd desperately been waiting to receive

out he pulled a medical card
containing the insignia
he had longed to place on his flimsy driver's license

a donor sticker...

in a life lost in selfishness and sin
his final act was to donate a body,
his body,
and in this way he was finally to become
a dandelion

in haste he said a prayer and slammed his
jaundice perceived body
down
into his garden of dandelion

the sudden and forceful movement
scattered the bumble bee yellow jackets
into a merciless frenzy
prompting a spectacle of stinging

lifeless he lay fully aware of his
deathly allergic reaction
to the golden striped honey bee

and with this he drifted to dream of a God his mother
holding him cradled

puckering a divine lip
blowing
his
donated
body
like
floating
embers
back
to

the
world
to seed in the hearts of the sick and pure

and a once fleshy snake skinned body
turned glittery gold
as the boy became one among many

a dandelion

15 min of fame

Like sunflowers in the rain
warm showers on marigold
my hangnails outgrow my fingers
in the maritime of incubating sleep

buoyant on the bed
a twin size lily pad
my two lower extremities flop over starboard
breaking the bones in upward current kicks

in saving
faces I don't recognize appear
like New York tugboats
possible strangers in the crowd
or people from another life
one time met

No time to choose

I grab a few in a game of chance
push the others over
capsizing my denials
taking solace in my self-proclaimed fact

"They're just wanna-be incubus"

Then sixteen minutes from getting to the bottom of this
my white stone eyes once again inherit pigment
growing green with covered moss
bringing life to dead
in a fifteen minute catnap over

but as usual
my labia lids stick together in rebirth
losing the fight with daily bouts of pink eye
as the dried in crustaceans of my weeping sleep

are forced apart with forceps fingers
only to be greeted
by an old friend named vertigo
as my equilibrium slips in the riverdance
over the cliff

the edge of my hydraulic hide-a-bed

cashmere carpet warmth

a tiptoe run on bikini waxed linoleum floors
is cold and unforgiving
but I press on to the weight change
in heels emergency landing
of your Cashmere carpet warmth

one thumbprint step closer to you
I evaporate in your foreshadow
saving me from the claustrophobia
of my own body taste
taking this chance
to bow to the battle of consequence

and I roll my Russian roulette eyes, point
and fire upon you
waiting for the connect
but cannot
reach past your radiating heat in the delay
because it's not enough

kind of like these thoughts

waving off a tactile tongue without the touch
an anticipation

in a
    panty sniff

can only take us so far

so let's finish each other off

because if not

hindsight's a hole in the heart
and I've been hollowed before

melancholy anomaly – the yin of my dream

urethra exhale
upward current spirits wind
starts the sprint of slithering splinters dredge
towards life's delicacy caviar uterus egg
where the race to be an anomaly
ends in a cul-de-sac
of gilled liquid amniotic oxygen
false imprisonment
a 9 month sentence of solitary confinement
in biology's speakeasy chemical brew
the preparatory rehabilitation (epi)center-stage
before the carnage of sociology fate placement
directly succeeding placenta burst
spawn

look who's on trial

three bites of the unusual
  leaves me suspect
& even if the evidence is circumstantial
  I'm still on trial

spilling self-incriminating dyslexia
  from a fungus on my tongue
brushing me with bristles against the grain
  on a brush dipped on a palette of shade

painting me a prism lacking sparkle
  as I walk
an overgrown fugitive child on busy streets
  seeing everything I should be

walking right by me
  and to the lay observer
on my skinny skeletal shell I'm an eerie calm
  like a Kenyan running a marathon

my viscera heart races on the inside
  to its demise
exhausted
  the toxins of my tired trying normalcy

like so many strangers lost
  I find comfort
in the emergency
  ambulance sirens and trauma

setting off exploding fire hydrants
  where I can jump in the white foam
and ride the river raft rapid
  through the gutter to the underworld

always
  I get stuck on the storm grate
waiting for friends
  as I'm left

an outlaw and a clairvoyant
  seeing with one eyed dyslexia

three moves ahead
  but always behind
and always towards the end

digital watch band-aids

in the anniversary of outgrowing wrists
shackled in tourniquet bracelets,
my pulse is just an hour-glass spasm
reaching for a rebel sun through open sores

the black blood dried in mid pour

and coarse are the scabs I love to wear,
but soft as me
in the pagoda skin they kiss to dress

my obsidian jewelry

outshines the brightest eruption
of horizontal light
at the bottom of any dark room door

tomato soup yum

alone at the midnight diner she orders:
an on purpose spill of tomato soup
inking an early white winter dress
because she's in denial
at the lack of punctuation
on her monthly sentence
a 3 month losing battle with
menopause
she confronts the almighty Albert Einstein
finding his time space continuum
in QVC anti-aging creams
a temporary fix
as she waits to retire
so she can lactate
her 401K on plastic surgery
erasing predisposed myths about her milfhood legend
the better ammunition
to seduce her son's
childhood friends

shoeless seahorses

a strangely sober mid-life aqua cowboy
on the oxygen bar of land searches for a new ride
asking with a three decade throat lozenged rebel yell
"where the fuck's the new wave?
somebody, please somebody,
tell me where the fuck's the new wave?"
but all to be seen were
shoeless seahorses stiffening their Mohawk manes
with Vaseline gel as they walked out of water
strutting the peerless strokes of punks
a generation past the grunge
pirating their lyrics from legend tongues

singing the chorus wrong and outta' tune

Bye Bye Miss American Pie
drove my pain to the needle
but the needle was dry
and dem' good ole boys
were thinkin' 60's and tie-dye
singing this'll be the day that I die

The Day the Music committed Suicide

dark monikers

lunger flung in throat clearing spit(e)

monikers, rancor, foul language
eavesdropped
from persons thought to be alone
shapeshift in my greeting presence

lesson learned

linguistics meant for no ears will always find a pair
and these are never to be ashamed of or unaccounted for

they're the ones I live to decipher

like my abnormal heart beat

strange, inefficient,   a little out of place

but keeping me alive

abstract caramel apple carnivals

carnival caramel apples
the red sand on cliffs
a summer sun showing
a tea cup cardiac catastrophe
looming on the horizon

watching
the lines amassing
wearing nothing
but nineteen29 clothing

upside-down
umbrellas

the only things they're holding
the left hands pointing down
the crowd begins a' cheering

"O' my God the sky is falling"

"O' my God the sky is falling"

Old money
New money
No money

Jump!

Old money
New money
Nobody

Jump!

& one by one they come a landing

flat

like souvenir carnival pennies

the red lily pads they're becoming
keeps children's hopes a floating
through an out of date life insurance policy

signed by

a human ink stain
marking man's undoing

we begin eating

carnival caramel apples
the red sand on cliffs
sliding bloody copper in loafers
the pennies for our future

macaroons

I have a dream
just a dream
a place of humble beginnings
a crumb dungeon of half eaten macaroons

Crayola stenciled
wax paper skies
template backgrounds
no oppressive lines

orange cookie sheet residues
wheat brazen

grass stained eyes

rainbow pit stains
on slogan shirts

it's a lot different here
but it's a lot the same

we don't touch what we want
we fear for what we have

life goes on

they'll say

see you on the inside

but don't forget
to say goodbye

just a dream

just unused skin
hiding
under patches
of playground jeans
stitched shut blow holes
suffocating child
end of my mammal

scream

self-serve smelling salts and
alarm clock heaters

just a dream

Elmwood café

as seven smoked Marlboros
pass unnoticed under lost
conversations of Elmwood café

peripheral vision leads me astray
allowing meeting of retina splendor
as aspirin thin boiling blood
streaks across naked veins
sparking heart beat arrhythmia

leaving lavender eyeliner dripping
into blue eyes sky
gazing mine penetrating
tan stars of face
an astrological sign
in freckly mosaic genetic lines

that predict my coming to you

rubbing them away

limber lasts the love to night
changing, morphing
walking,

to waltz   to halt

crustaceans dried
skeletal tears

sticking, crumbling
clinging
blending
absorbing

cousins to joy
come

full circle
here
creeping

to stop   to dead

a wake
performed
under sleeping eyes

carcinogenic the fragrance
          her

roses that wouldn't keep
roses that made her weep

carcinogenic the fragrance
          her

accidental voyeur

flaming wings turned to lungs
fangs made too long
a suicide survivor
screams forever

somewhere universes are colliding
confused
i've seen the pictures
they feed on each other
swapping circle stories
death conjured in hapless sex
colors mixing
in beautiful perish
and the offspring
they are the shooting stars
embarking once
the hopeful bastards
lost souls traveling

                          nowhere home

the poor empty space cadets
dark highway cadavers
in secret maybe
they ache to explode
but disintegration now does do
and the afterbirth trails
squirming a tails gleam
flaming
flapping a single wing
and minced
a lung pushes out a diving scream
a getaway
into lucky eyes
ones that shine
but never match the color

and the burn it dines
the black holes
of constricting pupils
another empty space
invaded
discovered
then gone

the suicide survivor
screams on
forever

confused

i've seen the pictures

his awake

Societal Specifics
expunge revolutionary vision
and somehow deems love
insufficient &

the trite repetition of life
clouds his ways
mismarks the days
until,
repletion kills his senses &

his awake became
                    an amputee's itch
nothing but manufactured bliss
he puts on his prosthetic face
gives his best half hitchhiker smile
closes his eyes
licks the stamps
places them on his lids
he mails himself away

::Enter::

an amniotic dream

he fingers the rosacea red sea
rides the ripple like liquid ladders
breaks the tangerine reflection
of a sun setting sky
until he can wade
                    to the beach
and roll around on the sandpaper coast till dusk

scratching itches
tearing stitches
making abrasions

a ruby red elixir
bleeding ambrosia tainted blood

the ambulatory visit
nears complete
he decides
        unilaterally
dry
   rinse
repeat

dry
   rinse
repeat

until
 his spider leg lashes tickle his brow
    crawling him conscious

then again

his awake became
                an amputee's itch.
nothing but manufactured bliss.
he puts on his prosthetic face
head to pillow
head to pregnant bed
he listens to the kicking dreams before they're born
last trimester
what's the sex?
what's the sex?
he puts on his prosthetic face
gives his best half hitchhiker smile
closes his eyes
licks the stamps
places them on his lids
he mails himself away

gone

through the dead black
of a manifest destiny
cross country trek
to the Atlantis
of new beginnings
I was driving an empty car
on an empty stomach
as I left my memories in taxidermy
somewhere on the west coast

and as the road became more bumpy
I was noticeably more edgy

until the no lights of Midwestern roads
made me a chain smoker
turning my cigarettes to orange flickering flashlights
pointing me to the believed point of day breaking

And as I rolled my window down ever so slightly
a
 s
  h
   i
    n
     g my Par-l(i)ament spotlights
I found the fear to match
of a similar friend
in the midnight screams of a crack windowed wind

I socket

2 green beanbag painted eyes
+ 1 red disintegrating sandpaper tongue

    (equals)

    3 perfect shots disguised in a clowns mouth *shocked*

 * The frizz of an electric socket *spark*
* In an open casket service display   *
   * Somewhere out on the fray *   *
  * Without the me looking out   *
   * Without the you looking in   *

& our love is electrocutions *tingle*   *
in multiple dimensions superposition | superposition
spli::ced by spinal extension cords embrace
that you stand to ruin by saying
                  *
"This feels weird, I think my arm just fell asleep~"
       *
I argue with cattle-prod smiling dismay
                                    *
"No hunny, your whole body's gone under"
           *
                                *
_____
 *

4 eyes fall into to each other's
   Open casket gaze
       *

47

on the other side

A certain deserter always hides in the green fertile forest—

a tree without leaves
    he stands
soul-less among the others
swaying
like a drunk man in the lukewarm liquid breeze
his naked limbs cackling as they rattle
like dead bones shifting in a plate tectonic grave

I'm enthralled
this tree speaks to me
if only figuratively
more than the colorful others
and as my visits become more conjugal
his courage tightens
like the top of a screw on salt shaker
after a childish prank

"You know,
there's a reason the only leaves I've ever had
were dead birds falling
with wings disappearing
before hit they hit the ground."

naturally frightened by the murmur of an inanimate
supposedly brainless object
my voice cracks
like a spider being broken under a stepping shoe

"WHAT?!?"
I said, half hoping for no response.

"I was born upside-down,
and all you see are stiff dry roots
reaching for the precious underground sun.
But if you promise
to be buried next to me,
when you die
you shall see
a world well beyond the lack
of a man-made so-called beauty."

this is the last and only time he spoke

I wrote it in my will—
when death comes around
I'll be buried on that hill
next to my friend
the dead looking tree
hoping there's another world
somewhere
on the other side
of upside-down

brother

swimming in a pool of embryonic fluid
diving to the depth, chasing black crucifix

I descend,
reach to touch it.
cut fingers plexiglass shavings
underwater world turns crimson
I suffocate-
liquidy casket

wading, waiting, impending death
I see my little angel fetal
un-blossomed flower
shedding petals

an unborn father
an unborn son

umbilical rope ascending
clutching tiny fingers wrinkled

to this day I wish I could have stayed

an unborn friend
an unborn heaven sent

mystically appearing fading transient
a memory constantly repeating

my angel,

the role you play so well
cast aside sadness dwell

an unborn brother

stillborn the story told
tiny hands my life they hold

guiding light unveiling direction
my mind your forever resurrection

our womb your tomb
my life, my brother
our love in bloom

maybe

sometimes I think I believe
sometimes I don't know what
and then I walk,
and then I wonder;

what's the Mexican mowing the lawn thinking
what's the bird on the wire singing,
surely, more than mating
surely, more than money
  what's the day worth dreaming -- maybe

then there's traffic, being pedestrian
                          I'm the only moving--
I wonder if we're evolving
or if inventions are stopping our bodies
  what's the day worth dreaming -- maybe

is creation happy-- that I'm not now
surely, more than -- would she?
no, I'm not bi-polar
just haven't quite turned,
                 that jagged little corner

yah,
sometimes I think I believe
sometimes I don't know what

but, I have become a fan of praying/meditating
surely, I don't know if it's working
but what's the harm in trying
   after all,
     what's the day worth dreaming --
                     without
                         all these little maybes

para dice

air tight, dead beaten, black, and broken
like a baby seal in chevron
the grand piano poses with its crumpled Bambi legs
top closed as an Amish woman's cleavage
staring back at me clear
like the shiny anorexic tip jar on the lounge singer's throat
after coughing up her whiskey syrup
tainted moans disguised as --- topless girls gone wild from
impanema
missing all the high notes
and hitting all the wrong ones
puberty without the celebrity
but with the spray on tan

no...no one's listening
no...no one's watching

except for me over your shoulder
all the while
poking you in the backside
with my green cactus pistachio shelled fingers
not realizing it hurts
pissdrunk
counting your white sheep teeth
falling asleep
on my french kiss tongue
waking tomorrow only to dive off the cheap hotel rooftop
like mary poppins with a hangover
floating with 1 little pink mai tai umbrella
survived by
"watching the medicine go down"
"watching the medicine go down"

aging primates

an aging primate in a space ship
I look down through
windows
round ones
which for some reason always seemed to be more
human
than rectangular and square ones

and I see Earth

casually spinning in precision pirouettes
as I am also dancing
with the gracefulness of gravity gone
at the idea of home growing

smaller and smaller and smaller

and in the background I hear
Russian and English
voices garbled and yelling
through the dated Oregon Trail
of green and black computers

Houston is surely pissed that I am pressing buttons

but I fooled them in acting dumb
call me a monkey stowaway
but I've seen Charlie and the Chocolate Factory
a thousand times
and I know when you're in a Wonkavator

press the red button
press the red button
press the red button

no matter how many there are

content with three or four
I suspend reclined
my hairy arms tucked to a fluffy pillow
behind my hollow head
and I drift and drift
in MY hijacked spaceship
realizing
I'm nothing
just
a child's balloon
floating
with the dreams left in the hands of its outreaching owner
on an adventure
through a black distant sea
munching the stars for plankton
brushing my teeth with food from tubes
unconcerned for the moment
that i don't know how to land

full speed ahead

you don't need to know the end

sabbatical

on Sabbatical from the shackles of houses storm
I was not alone walking the sidewalk corridor
in the break of the cold winter rain
                              slightly ahead,
I saw his frizzy unkempt hair hanging from his grey beret
showcasing sweet chocolate streaks of youthful black
pinned against the drop
of a maturing scalp succumbing to the preference
of a more sophisticated taste in subtle vanilla clumps

chasing his snail tracks I could see his frail shell
as he stood slightly bent
 ---------------------------his posture like an owl on a branch
surveying the ever-changing world
as he held his pipe like a walking stick
close to his face
safe keep for the journey
shuffling
crisp oxygen breaths with mouthfuls of
Indian tobacco taste
as each littered inhale from carefully carved question mark
Sherlock woody
stoked the fire
doubling its chamber as a crematorium
turning our attention to the funeral of ghost-soul exhales
in cloudy evaporating memories
leaving withered
from the tapestry of his grimacing, wheezing lungs
And from his long stares tailgating the smoke to heaven
it was easy to believe the shapes and forms of these misty
holograms carried special meaning to the man
desperately I wanted to borrow his wiry circle spectacles
to decode the fading encryptions
but deep down I knew
acumen like that
rarely, if ever, comes that cheap

and anyway
it was time to pass him by

as much as I longed to hunt the wisdom of
his skeleton key, snakeskin shedding years
through the probing of endless poaching questions

the fact of the matter was and still is
I have yet to learn to walk that slow

so for now
I'll just have to bathe in the sweet smell
of the wet liquid asphalt
and the creep of its reflection
in the suns unforgiving afterglow

Caligula

hide all the trepidation
in a cum shot to your own face
the blind side of
a hit and run
penis gun
the ultimate degradation
in a multiple choice answer to
plastic surgery, bulimia,
a gym rat vision of grandeur
the overall escaped version
of the reincarnation of Rome¡ s Caligula
spawning this century¡ s mass spread
of fornication
      megalomania
        -Masturbate onto mirrors!
        -Masturbate onto mirrors!
because you know you're the only thing
that's gets you hard
because you know you're the only thing
that gets you wet
                so come on let him lead the rave
spew new life onto your empty carcass
bathe in your own secretions
the final act of the pumping
Vain, Vain, Vain
        -Masturbate onto mirrors!
        -Masturbate onto mirrors!
he screamed one more time
faintly remembering hearing
somewhere vinegar
disintegrates pearls

and promptly
he was lost in a swallow

fickle

fickle foul is the mouth of a pony tail held by a ghost
drooling the slurs of a twin and its tongue
in a language learned
forgone
by another bequeathed-

these, the hallucinations
of the mean

speak as memories

left in light shadows
shining in the dark
passing as assassins of being in retractable truths
closing as I find them opening
without the slightest stench of the beast
I,
2X man
I,
1X alien

We are we again

I plead
cast aside you demons dwell
the matriarch is on the prowl
cyanide drip the crying ok
for what you did
intuitive
as the beat of cardiovascular drum

cataclysms in the prisms kiss of cliffs

the mist
   the kiss of cliffs
     disintegrating from
      cleft
         lip of legend

 window dressing poets
 ashing ash tray thoughts
   spawn names to tattered dreams
    a momentary place to slave

      in the wet regret of ocean waves

      penciled memories

        sculpted handsome indecision

        A calming force
       yours, mine
        divine
         the cleft lip of God
         the cool kiss of cliffs
        we reason
         religion

         disappear

           window dressing poets
           wish

           solstice

unaware for once of body
welcome known to the abundance
of drying water

cataclysms caught in prism

triangular planet
squeezing out rainbows
white light traversing the black
satellites on the way
to another home

know it

triple sec
impaired mindspeak
impaled on the bedpost

with your cowardice prowess
you found me

lying at the edge of death
fetal
tear-stained empathy

morphine drip
with a lemon twist

disguise me a ventriloquist

doll

sucking on the inside out flowers

don't try
but you will
there's no way you could see
past the peace signs in your eyes

a retractable tulip tongue
dodges ripped up philosophy
pre-emptive God's son
in all its in-formidable glory

a useless device
that had its taste
then lost its chance

somewhere in the blankness
of the wood hiding behind the white

a red bloody candy cane
impaled on the bedpost

you found me

information

I see Jesus on every one—
avatars for all time
mildly bloodshot eyes
striped like candy canes in their final having look

there's something glorious about dying—
    with open eyes
those are the real ghosts
the morphing immortals
in revolving door odysseys
the frozen satellites of open tear

o' to the wooden crosses holding power lines

I see Jesus on every one—
linked un-flown kites
electrical umbilical cords
fizzing crowns of thorns
piercing, spewing fossil brains
information—

where do you go to die?

in my head
in yours
resurrected in different forms

everything is touching me
almost too much handle

the sunlight fakes on its brother moon
the full candle disappearing in its cycle
séances performed in troubled dreams
hums of concentration
        nothing
but gargled thoughts

burned to cash in oblivion
                    mouths (open sores in need of stitches)
their powder keg crematorium

everything is touching me
almost too much to handle

infinite possibilities
millions of hands
millions of thoughts
circling me
circling you
spinning minds and bodies turn to Ouija boards
tattooed numbers and letters on feathered souls
stopping and starting too fast
    building an answer that cannot last

 o' to the wooden crosses holding power lines

I see Jesus on every(-)one
it is worth repeating

there's something glorious about dying—

        with open eyes

but information
o' so lonely

where do you go
where do you go when you have to d...

Grandma's goodbye

her fountain of youth was an RV destination desert
where miles were logged on an unplugged speedometer
and the days were counted down in a Monday to Sunday
pillbox
leaving |S|M|T| |T|F|S| Wednesday empty
as she threw her head back
the hammer on a revolver gulping water
swallowing
gelatin coded prescriptions and her last bit of nutrition
but in the end the calcium never could quite catch up
while her spine retracted
like a slinky
on the last step down
an
ancient
   Mayan
      pyramid
         staircase
leaving her appearance smaller
but her legend bigger
and although
she was losing a battle with gravity
she was winning her final hand of solitaire
spooning her last meal
her favorite dessert
the purple and orange of rainbow sherbet
a 10 minute summer Arizona Sunset

straps

swollen, pensive

insatiable regret in the passing of time

linger I

on the roads of feelings

paying tolls with totalitarian coins

just expired gun powder pushed into a civil war musket

mull I

the entrance to the crypt keeper's garden

taking precious moments to hide

in the showering shadow of fiery leaves of ferns

blousing

teasing I

with slices

of

blinding

Venetian

light

God

You are so contagious

but why am I

so immune?

violence in vaccine

sacrifice in a long walk

insatiable regret of passing time

God

You are so contagious

but why am I

so immune?

straightjackets

made for us

to give ourselves hugs

hells bells jingle in the rubbing of their undone straps

linger I

on the roads of feelings

paying tolls with a pocketful of totalitarian coins

God

I killed you for your skin
You tiger

You lemon

You endangered

Venetian

with the uneven spread

of your

Slices of light

God

You are so contagious

but why

amInsolovewithyou?

so immune

straightjackets

made for us

to give ourselves hugs

listless the longer

they've come to bare
mauve flowers and crimson clovers
petrified white stone tongues
that lick alive the air

talking
obituaries

I read them

like newspapers

a little hard turning the page
a little afraid of
an unused lot

right over there

a grounded pirate
dancing in the fog

listless the longer
to become

an out of water
prairie dog

so excuse me
excuse me for

kicking down tombstones
and replacing them with mirrors

because it's time
time to face the hate
that muddy little choice
I've been waiting to make

stay and play today
or run

run so far away

a grounded pirate
dancing in the fog

yellow

splintered rhetoric foams out the mouths
of political shamans
the most important humans?
one yellow rose spreads its petals
slowly, like an angry fist
giving in to wrinkled peace of palm
and in near perfect spring bloom
its white hearts give
temporary color calls
like a mousetrap hug
R
  a
   z
    o
     r
    b
   l
   a
  d
e

ladder
every thorn on its stem has a bee
       impaled on it
face first
stingers still intact
pollen on twitching insect fingers
windblown to oblivion
allergic honey madness sticking
to ghost memories
driven to beauty
to hang themselves on it
like a self-portrait on a bedroom wall
to kill themselves on it
like misfiring white cells in fake diseases' squall

to know nothing else
to know nothing else
without ugly conclusion
souls dancing in the breeze
like errant blown kisses
of queens

gelling

black and white, hard to see
my shut eyes hide under ultrasound jelly
I dream in sonograms

the slight glimpses of uninhabitable spaces
temporarily inhibits until the realization
that my loneliness is measured by the love or hate
I have for myself
and not by who or what is the fill around me

but even this has become a diabolical barometer
since the epiphany
that my surroundings are me and I am my surroundings

flying? or floating in waves?
the faces and shapes that appear
I do not recognize
I now only give a name
no separate categories
just drops that drip from an invisible cerebellum umbrella
to meet again in evaporations or oceans.

this is Love-
in efficacy non-judgmental

but being human I feel forced into judgments
not until I kill the human inside of me
virally disintegrating it without mourning
eating away at its transparent umbrella
like disease vs. disease
will I drip into the black ocean again
vacuumed by choice?

I dream in sonograms
in infinite possibilities

hanger

Another ske
Ust   let
J   on
                   In
                   The
        World's
        Clo
        Set
My collar bone has become nothing, but
A clothes hanger   With a brain
For hook   looking
        For a new dream
                To
                Hang
                On
                To

mahogany heart sleeve

My Eyes are scabs ripped off repeatedly
by an alkaline acid battery brain
melting on to a vitamin D deficient, coffee stained skin
asphyxiating from second hand black breath sputtering
me into a psychedelic closet of claustrophobia

I sit, in a backless chair,

regurgitating sawdust swallowed
to sponge my insides from leaking out onto Xerox paper

contemplating a holocaust of love
wearing a mahogany heart barcode on my sleeve
so you know where to stab it

sway

diving under liquid curtain lids
dreaming behind the scene
sleeping eyes twitch back and forth

watching the pendulum swing

& you run to one side
to stop its sway
but before you
know it's gone away
                |
                |
                |
    so I say to you
the unconscious

        meet me in the middle

        we'll hop on there
          & go for a ride
          to the dead ends
        of golden grass beyond
          & it's there
          we'll stay
          & it's there
          we'll play
        till it's TIME to pass away

        or slip awake

motel sex

cuz we were--
sippin' n' drinkin'
in counter-clockwise rotation
laughin' n' tokin'
& roastin' the holy ghost
boxin' the motel room

complainin'
it smelled like sex
without the mirrors
complainin'
it smelled like death
without the fear

cuz we were-

rollin' joints with King James
when she said:
"God damn!"
"David and Judas you burn way too fast"

but that didn't stop us, not a chance

cuz we were-

slippin' n' slidin' our razorblade tongues
pumpin' n' thumpin' our pelvic thrusts
dancin' n' lancin' on the bed
lickin' n' feedin' each other's blood
cryin' - cubic zirconias
watchin' 'em hit the rug
ripplin' n' turnin' our minds to dust

complainin'

the room smelled like disease
without the bugs
complainin'
the room smelled like us without the drugs

calico

the thoughts of a calico escape

as archeologists brushes
do a gentle dust
they paint the life a of a glittered tomb
& the lost thoughts of a calico escape
in a cute cat meow
that hides the anger of a lion
in a 5-point Egyptian triangle
mummified
till the violence of long waited release
rips the dressing off covered wounds
like two opposite strips of velcro
shred
exposing the lack of feeling
in hemoglobin-less dried blood
that's soaked the skin for ages
turning it corduroy
like fingertips wrinkled
out of salt rimmed glass tub
bathed in red
a strong strawberry daquiri
escape

the lost thoughts of a calico

archeologists brushes
do a gentle dust
paint the life of a glittered tomb

the thoughts of a calico

claiming the left
is the right brain
reciprocal

the intentions of an emotional calico
blend
grave robbers

choreographed

choreographed like married sex
I follow my thoughts down the road again
embarrassed of a few
I pretend they're not my own
but it's useless because it's obvious
we're wearing double ended nooses
so none of us carries the burden
of pulling leashes
a cruel and unusual way to teach us

& the stretch marks showing around the collar
isn't necessarily evidence we've grown
just maybe that we have different homes

tired of all this sun

my brain feels like its performing
an angioplasty on my skull
a black balloon
floating
with one thought repeating

an occasional ache to be the same

farmers market

the mercantile is buzzing with cross pollination
as farmers and pickers spread their full Indian weaves
with rainbow tear ducts in irrigating delight

milkworts and legumes
tulips and prune
flowers and seeds
nectars and juices flowing
      to and fro fertile and tropical seas

ode this be to the green and floral canopy
where the minestrone and sherbet is stirred
to mix
in ripe aphrodisiacs and magical spells
****
and batting be thinning the lashes of daughters'
                  and princesses' eyes
plucked and puckered in blow dart kisses
puncturing and defrosting a cold veggie
artichoke heart
as once the Wichita lonely
is now smiling in penitent pastels
without the vice of killing disguise
    disintegrated to snow dust
the ice cones of once
              carnivorous eyes

ciggy fingers

Dipping my unlubricated fingers into your

tobacco leaf dry red box

of Marlboros

suffering the satisfaction agony of a last rut

pondering why

my fingers smell like cigarettes

when they could smell like you

I reach again

Dipping my unlubricated fingers into your folding box

of matches

ripping the last one inhaling and blowing

secondhand glazed donuts of smoke

penetrating them selfishly

with my sticky butterscotch lollypop mind

pondering why

my fingers smell like cigarettes

when they could smell like you

Crimson Cabernet

Red love letters
Drip Raspberry Cream
Melting eyelids scarlet.
Sunset revealed
Burning luminescent
Sedentary flame,
we became
One
Through
Transfusion.
M
i
x
i
x
n
g

Strawberry blushes and bloody head rushes,

Sipping from crystalline wine glasses

of Crimson Cabernet.

sew the marsupium

the child's mind is a marsupial
a delicate body
birthing the inherit good of a human soul
to store in an empty well-groomed parental pouch
but
his growing baby eyes deceive

sucking the violence out of life
2 hungry corneal leeches
performing surgery to suture the opening
left open, barely,
by an 11 year old
who bought his first gun in a video game
raping his virginity slowly
losing the romanza and innocence of an Aborigine
in puberty

but some would say his destiny was to lose

there's only violence in the news

and now
he just wants to leave

and now
we watch him without a cry

steady as he goes
where martyrs go
to die

and now
we watch him without a cry

steady as he goes
where martyrs go
to die

is this paradise?
is this paradise?
is this paradise?

3 left questions whispered in the distance

Nam

walking by
I fed the hungry man a stare
but not nearly enough to fortify
his crippled appetite

wildly
he rolled his way over
with wheelchair bulging biceps
no doubt the product of muscles migrating north
from the atrophy in his legs

and before I could say a...

out he pulled a gun
and squeezed the trigger click
till all I heard was—
!BANG!

frozen
I became the paraplegic
waiting on the exit wound
until I saw the black and white flag dangle
        half mast
out of his looney tunes plastic gun

then in sneak attack
between my careless blink
his gun-less machete calloused hand
grabbed and ruffled the dark jungle
of my hairy arm

mildly frightened
I looked up at his whiskey weathered face
allowing our eyes to meet
with that cold somber soldiers harrowing embrace

and in the whites
of his rice paddy gaze
I could see him see me
circling in his condor brain

*strapping lad
*mid 20's
*shaved head
*camo pants
*with a cocoa butter tan

and the tear forming from the corner of his mind
found
the corner of his eye
and as it dropped slowly
stopping to suspended animation

I saw it turn to flame
just before touching ground
burning up my spine
like a trip wire line
as I became the napalm
of his today

neglected are the souls with holes
punctured
by fruitless wars
and wretched
be the ones that fail to recognize
them
leaving sidewalks and underpasses
unkempt and unempty
at any time
day or night

Elizabeth's wish

Elizabeth was a dreamer
but she wasn't the only one
as she watched her last lonely Lincoln
fighting to float
descending out of focus
a copper feather
down to the depths
of a dead president
metallic reflecting sea

"Whatcha wishing for honey?"
Her mother asked half-heartedly
paying more attention to the next task of her lengthy day

"Nothing mommy."
Elizabeth said hiding in reply
masking her careful whisper
so one else could hear
to make it null

"Wishing well o' wishing well
i wish, i wish -
for no child
like or not like me
to ever or forever
again go hungry"

And as soon as the wish was done
Elizabeth was gone
and the day turned to night
where the thieves and bums
could work their work
without the bitter embarrassment
of a lemon yellow sun

Enter

Charlie starving

A witty drunk
who never could seem to catch
a businessman's break
as he was losing
a lifetime quarrel
with a God stealing daughter
a week short of her 21st birthday

he lived
on dollar menus and cheap acid reflux booze
frequenting city park fountains
plucking peoples dreams in many pennies
and little silver
compiling
enough scratch to eat and be a fish
for yet another
lackluster self-serving day

yet shortly
after Charlies slamming
of soaked pocket change
on the first fast food counter
he was wiping ketchup from his vagabond beard
on his polished burger wrapper
feeling quasi-content with what briefness he had
in satiety slash sobriety

while somewhere

for no reason to her recollection
Little Elizabeth

couldn't stop herself from smiling

crazy is

questions creeping into a blue sky
like the peripheral catch
of distant wings on a faraway raven
playing rendezvous with the back of my mind
nearsightedness left to make fuzzy plans for
future
abominable wretchedness born to be aborted
artificial insemination
cackles its way out of superstition
in catatonic laughs of hyperbolic hyenas
conjuring nervous comedy out of failed attempts
in finding ends in never starts
your fingers comb the hospital smell
out of my hair
hope plays matriarch
I'll live in your chest
And crazy is...
the reason behind finding the ampersand
between me & me
And crazy is...
the cyanide saliva left on our lips
the remnants of french kiss suicide tongues
And crazy is…
            'nt living
And crazy is...
the aberration of artificial insemination in me

wishes

a snow globe's on its head
the atmosphere's the glass
I look down for
fingerprints that aren't my own

the days they shake
my worlds they wait
to nights welcome back

Earth's right side up

stars flake spirits dandruffs fall
the end of inverted pirouettes
ballerina's blistered toes cooled

my hands held together tight
mistaken for praying
but they're really just mimicking

unsuccessful attempts at holding water

I try to catch them all

entanglement becoming part of the (w)hole

disintegrating smiles rain to frown
10 empty parking spaces in succession

once, you thought you found the new ground
but your search for undiscovered colors ends

& from the cavity evacuated
consciousness drips
heart shaped macadamia tears

the part of you that splashes
hides tidy in unheard echoing ripples
buried under rainbow grease stain rugs
left from another that has parked
then driven away

and you begin,
a part of you left in all layers,

your slow but steady rise to the top

remember

there is reflection in the prism
if you can make it to the other side

asexual

Sugar free without the sticky
my mind is sharp but languid
flowing as I swim in satellite dishes
chasing my libido
with high octane waving
sperm tailed dolphin kicks
through snippets in flashes
of clockwork orange advertisements-

I'm a man.

                              You're a woman.

I'm A MAN!

                              You're a woman

Alright, alright!!!

I'm a lesbian
I'm a closet cross-dresser
secretly wearing women's underwear
hiding a full grown uterus
The final Installment of the Feminist movement
Woman's lib
Civil war complete

Product : Epidemic sized Androgyny

I'm a man.

                              You're a woman.

I'm A MAN.

You're a woman.

Alright, alright

I'm a lesbian.
A Bisexual   an Asexual
With an STD forced into me
fulfilling societies
drawkcaB evolution
To self-reproduction

crawling out of child safety bottles
through an ajar medicine cabinet mirror
staring back into it
crying and arguing unconvincingly

You said you never thought of yourself that way.
Bullshit,

Everyone is gay!"

No, you said you never thought of yourself that way.
Bullshit,

Everyone is gay!

"Go Fuck yourself!"

I already did
-twice today.

asexual fantasies
fulfilling societies
drawkcaB evolution
to self-reproduction
asexual Fantasies

the harlots answer
to epidemic sized androgyny

all from swimming in Satellite Dishes
sifting through the snippets in flashes
of clockwork orange adverts

sleep falls to the rising sun

delicate and pleasant
a scream caught in her stare
sentiments without sentences
words,
thoughts
without the air

performances these
   still/born
rare and rare...

 sunbathed n' drenched
   night wrinkles,
burns from off the moon
 skin turns
    the break of day

halting --slowly spinning
  her thoughts a golden crank
an ailing in her chest
   just a box of toys

   wind instruments
   red piped organs
   blue vein
         ivy flutes

on they play   only
     as sonnets
masquerading
to the   awaiting
   of fateful donors

slightly breathing now
 as death imagined
begins its teething
 dreamings

all still and silent

sleep falls as she goes

up to the sunrise again

somewhere inside my intelligence

Mama,
Today i got lost in my intelligence
And i forgot
 how i always have a choice in my reaction
And i forgot
 how my emotions are more than chemicals described by
science
And i forgot
 how it was the first time i ever got scared
And i forgot
 how happy was all that was ever really there
And i forgot
 how exactly to be   alone
And i forgot
 how i never really am
And well
Mama,
can you tell me that story again
you know the one you always said
 how i didn't even cry while n' after i was being born
And well
Mama,
can you tell me that story again
you know the one you always said
 how my first word was a little laugh inside a tiny smile
And well
Mama,
can you tell me that story again
you know
the one you always said
 how angels ceased to exist until my closed baby blues
 first met your honey lips
because well
Mama,
Today i(t) got lost somewhere deep inside my intelligence

teachers of dreams

the teachers of dreams stammer
fumbling with their own
could the cursor blink any faster?

misnomers in beauty I've tuned them out
dialing into radio faces and brains
wafting wading
transparent in frequency
the familiarity in and between species

I bend with the waves
as I blend with their emissions
viscosity breakdown in the fusion—
these thoughts they don't bleed
and it's hard to accept
but some need to see
so we cut ourselves together

sanguine

same in the flow
scars for braille
pity the necessity of this mnemonic device

violence
& death

the only breeder
of pedigree hope?

the teachers of dreams stammer
in the arabesque coating of their own

still I wonder
could the cursor blink any faster?

the light under door

all alone darkness
can't sacrifice
the images of self
that vaunt
honeycombed memories
honeycombed memories honeycombed memories
honeycombed memories honeycombed memories
honeycombed memories
of insect eyes

convulsions in lids
their yellow rubbed twitch
pounce-
pounce as plastic rain boots
stepping over mire
tear duct
matchbooks
that have an end
putting out cleansing fire

what is lost that isn't gained?

pain

a black and white candy cane

striping, emerging on different levels
light at the bottom of multiple doors

one down horizontal I lay to see

another eye
staring back at me

the white
the iris
I fight through its tempting I
peer through its daunting

reflection

there is another

we have each other?

weltering eyes drip
feigning hope
puddle of tears form
a congregation past the fake
they touch under the door

Pangea

it's real

we wallow here
half past forever
in the river of our wet

sad, sad song

to forget
the barrier in our togetherness

walls of her boudoir

walls of her boudoir
were stenciled in black with shadows
remnants of her first botanical dream
and with swaying its crush
silence of dusk tempted me
as I began to wander
searching alone
dark in her made-up garden

when suddenly-

a maritime breeze hissed its kiss,
light brushed the orbiting room
and rainbows thought to color everything spinning
turning the small crystal balls
hanging my lovely's favorite rain
to fade-away stars
pure from the cloud white ceiling
in which they so happily came

I turned my gaze back to her
and whispered,
my breath gently pushing blonde inside her ear-

"sunrise, sunrise my darling"

but as certain as the morning came nothing
except
her lovely, familiar, peaceful sigh
and as usual
I decided that was fine
because I couldn't love anything more
than watching her dream
wandering beside her

in and out of sleep

entanglement

through a labyrinth of maize and brunette cowlicks
I glide down easily on circular stairway banisters
through scalp fields of varying lengths of hair

& with each galvanizing descent
I rise back up again
through addicts undertow
to the tips of white lips
the crashing conductor waves
breaking over telepathic lies

& I round them
like sharp coral stones over time
trading the warp of degenerated memories
for the momentum and power
of positive stimulation
in the brain tickling
of centipede intentions

waking early

the horizon smiles casually as it stretches
a contortionist's calm
lazily expanding
a cute kitten yawn

its calico colors strife the fight
in cotton candy clouds
half eaten to make their mark

the pinks and reds of a lost sailor's dawn

I walk (Dourghtey Rd.)

forming walls
blanketing eyes
cloaking dreams
civilizations built
bordered by serpentine masonry
the slippery barrier
offering optical illusion in beauty for boundaries
I see through intentions of conniver of civilizations new

I walk in the shadow of the hawk

those eyes mine
negate the covers
while the world remains colossal
and together we hover
nourish on the serpentine masons
devouring walls
bombing barriers
laying eggs, the shells, the only walls we have breaking

I walk in the shadow of the hawk

military burial

Mama's mind drifted into space
a shady crevice
from the everlasting summer
of Sunnis and Shiites

dreaming,
she solicits her baby's face
through sandy showers of pain

she sings:

"Oh say can you see?"
this (un)just wasn't meant to be

ears ring:

"The bombs bursting in air"

strapped to a car

strapped to a human heart chest

we confess
our love
through different books
only to the same God

dreaming,
she's drowning in a Baghdad quicksand
of hypocrisy exclaiming
"Democracy!!...Democracy!!
"Blasphemy!!"
"Blasphemy!!

because now she's the woman

forced to wear the black veil,

as tears roll silent off a silk satin face

saturating the trinity of a triangular American flag

bent,
folded,
and creased

like the edges of her shrinking heart

I to VI your classical critique of me

I

This is where I tell you
about a leaf falling
and how it relates to the meaning of life
in some over glorified
hidden metaphor
   written in vernacular technicolor
borrowed like sugar
from a neighbor
   named
   Thesaurus

II

This is where I tell you
that American English teachers preach
quality comes in length
   and that a good piece is judged only
by a new pen running out of ink
but I say
anyone can write filibuster with a trident
three lines
   at
   a
   time
you know sometimes
   there is magic in the brief

III

This is where I tell you
about some obscure story
from the good book
    or another boring literary classic
    or a buried quote from Foucault
    or another carcass philosopher
    proving my education
to give you ample reason for your
edification of my defecation (see # 1)
better yet this is where
I'll sneak in a snippet from Greek Mythology
Yah'
that seems to be in style

IV

This is where I tell you
something that has absolutely no meaning
and is weird for the sake of being weird
because that's how sophisticates identify art
in their good taste
and it's how to be original if you don't have
the time or patience
    to waste

V

This is where I tell you
that I like poetry amateur
    like porn
for there's always something to be said
in the girl next door
unless of course she becomes a star
for it's the idiosyncrasies of the average
that keeps me coming back
    furthermore

VI

This is where I tell you
you can finally stop reading
if you haven't already

Devil's contraceptive

your eyes are islands
with Lilliputian pupils
between squinting lids
lapping waves of dust
keeping them dry
as you cry
boulders for tears
seeds to be buried
deep in the desert sand you create
to grow and sow
another human heart

only this time you realize
you cannot

desolation is a fascination we all must endure
it's a phantom fish at the end of a lure
where you're the bait that no one bites
and your eyes
                        Islands
dormant volcanoes
waiting and waiting to swallow the world
in lava red
the color of love turned to charcoal
raining
raining
ash
in a storm of repetition
representing the human condition
the Devil's contraceptive

thank you

through the tiny holes of a retired hemp necklace
I see the neglect of college days

a place where I went to buy an education
and spent more money on drugs

and now my mind is a transistor radio

scouring channels
scanning frequencies
picking up tiny voices

anywhere from

dead dictators to
love letter poets

anywhere from

hippies to
yuppies

a dial searching to find a balance
in empty coffee house virtues

I often find myself repeating

"God is dead, God is dead, God is dead!!"

thanks a lot you asshole Friedrich Nietzsche

God is....

$$$$Acid Flashback$$$$

I once had a dream
back and to the left
back and to the left

that I was in Dallas
in the seat of old Jackie Onassis
catching JFK's brain
and putting it into mine

O' where O' where have the idealists gone

so it seems they all get shot
whether it's someone else's doing or their own

Just Cobain pessimism

I guess

$$$$$End flashback$$$$$

I digress

God isn't dead he's just
lost on the souls that try to make him/her/it
everything and everything
and nothing else nothing

and like a single shoe on the side of the highway
the rest of us are left alone watching
life pass goodbye
just because we have the audaciousness to ask why?

Fuck it

Let's just be arsons and burn ourselves
because in the end we are our own fuel

I'll only come to you when I can't find a light

(God)

I don't feel like killing you just yet

but,

if it's true what John Lennon says

"God is just a way in which we measure pain"

I still ask

Jesus Christ!?!?!
How much more do I have to take?!?!

Yes,

Thank you Nietzsche
Thank you Lennon
Thank you Jesus

You've all fucked me in the psyche

and I liked it

Amen

why I write

Unaware modern day avatar strums in midnight bedroom silence
----
on azure strings of a 30 lined binder paper guitar
----
popping the air blisters of a bubble wrapped heart
----
sealed in its shelter for its abstinence in feel,
----
releasing,
----
stale trapped halitosis latent Lamaze breaths of demons
----
through reverberation of pencil pick scratches
----
and dark timbre truths of eraser shavings spores
----
swimming tadpoles of dead ideas in their tail slithering adventures
----
to their wiping off to the floor
----
and as these prior cranial reincarnations settle for friends with the
----
"good"
----
in the wake of their re-birthing divorce

I'm almost forced to edit their hidden micro-phoned voice,
----
choking it off like a woman with black hole throat cancer
----
performing fellatio on an uncircumcised dildo
----
through the self-inflicted slit of her un-sterile stoma
----

but I don't

----

for the sake of my sanity

----

for the sake of my reality

I struggle to hear the speech and song

----

for the sake of me, I feel

A bit Uned_ted

----

murmurs of those we hold close

in the doldrums of speaking skies
winds wilt in imaginary lines
and hawks write home
wings dipped   in white ink cloud
gliding flapless
no hesitation
engaging blue
interweavings of heavens shroud

silent
apt
torn in curvature
murmurs
to all its own

    or more?

an acquiesce maybe
an ageless calligraphy

taught unspoken and shared adorn
written

to eyes that dream
but never closed

taught unspoken and shared adorn
written

to eyes that dream

but never closed

About the Author

Lee Pricer lives "on a mote of dust suspended in a sunbeam".

NeoPoiesis: *a new way of making*

1) in ancient Greece, poiesis referred to the process of making: creation - production - organization - formation - causation

2) a process that can be physical and spiritual, biological and intellectual, artistic and technological, material and teleological, efficient and formal

3) a means of modifying the environment and a method of organizing the self, the making of art and music and poetry, the fashioning of memory and history and philosophy, the construction of perception and expression and reality

4) an independent publisher with a steadfast goal to print and promote outstanding poets, writers and artists that reflect the creative drive and spirit of the new electronic landscape

NeoPoiesisPress.com